Joy!

A Bible Study on Philippians for Women

Keri Folmar

Cruciform Press | Released June, 2012

To my husband:
We may not do "light and funny" but marriage,
family, and ministry with you is truly a joy.

To Ruth, Chloe, and Andrew:
You are precious gifts from God. I love you.

To the ladies of the United Christian Church of Dubai:
Studying the Bible and being in community with you
has brought me great joy!

– Keri Folmar

CruciformPress

CruciformPress.com | info@CruciformPress.com

"This study points the way into the biblical text, offering a clear and effective guide in studying Paul's letter to the Philippian church. Keri Folmar encourages her readers first and foremost to listen well to God's inspired Word." — **Kathleen Nielson***

"Keri's Bible study will not only bring the truths of Philippians to bear upon your life, but will also train you up for better, more effective study of any book of the Bible with her consistent use of the three questions needed in all good Bible study: Observation, Interpretation, and Application." — **Connie Dever***

"Keri lets the Scriptures do the talking! No cleverly invented stories, ancillary anecdotes, or emotional manipulation here. Keri takes us deeper into the text, deeper into the heart of Paul, deeper into the mind of Christ, and deeper into our own hearts as we pursue Christ for joy in all things. Each new week of study provides a review of the previous week, to help us keep in context what we've studied. The subsequent days are for gold digging, and there are rich treasures to discover as we unfold the truth that our joy ultimately comes from glorifying God in every sphere and circumstance of life. I highly commend this study for your pursuit of joy." — **Kristie Anyabwile***

"Keri Folmar is convinced that God is God-centered and that for the sake of our joy, we should be, too. This inductive study will increase your joy in a loving God who is sovereign over all things. I highly recommend that you embark on this study with some other ladies. Then you can all watch in amazement at how God gives you contentment in him as he shows you the surpassing worth of knowing Christ Jesus as Lord." — **Gloria Furman***

See endorser bios at page 4.

Table of Contents

Endorser Bios

Kathleen Nielson is author of the *Living Word Bible Studies*; Director of Women's Initiatives, The Gospel Coalition; and wife of Niel, who served as President of Covenant College from 2002 to 2012.

Connie Dever is author of *The Praise Factory* children's ministry curriculum and wife of Mark, senior pastor of Capitol Hill Baptist Church and president of 9Marks.

Kristie Anyabwile is a North Carolina native and graduate of NC State University with a degree in history. Her husband, Thabiti, serves as Senior Pastor of First Baptist Church, Grand Cayman, and as a Council Member for The Gospel Coalition.

Gloria Furman is a pastor's wife in the Middle East, a Crossway author, and editor for the Domestic Kingdom blog.

This book is also available...

- In bulk discount pricing for as few as 6 copies
- In printable PDF format for $5.45
- Through our ebook licensing program (6 pricing levels)

Learn more at **bit.ly/JoyStudy**

(See the back pages of this book for more great titles from Cruciform Press.)

Joy! - A Bible Study on Philippians for Women

Print / PDF ISBN: 978-1-936760-56-5

As we begin this study of the Apostle Paul's letter to the Philippians, we should think through why we are studying the Bible. Why not read some other book? Or why not just get together with some ladies and chat?

Well, have you heard about the kindergarten teacher who had her class paint pictures of anything they chose? One little girl was working intently on her painting. After observing the girl for a moment, the teacher asked, "What are you painting?" The girl responded, "It's a picture of God." Amused, the teacher informed her, "No one knows what God looks like." Without looking up from her painting the little girl responded, "They will in a minute."

This might be a cute example of a precocious child, but many people paint pictures in their own minds of how God looks and acts. They "know" that God is a certain way because they want him to be that way. However, God is transcendent. That means he is beyond our capacity to know. First Timothy 6:16 declares God to be unique, the one "who alone has immortality, who dwells in unapproachable light, whom no one has ever seen or can see." God existed before time. He is the creator, and we are his creatures.

Thankfully, God has revealed himself and wants us, his creatures, to know him. Jeremiah 9:23-24 says:

> Thus says the Lord: "Let not the wise man boast in his wisdom, let not the mighty man boast in his might, let not the rich man boast in his riches, but let him who boasts boast in this, that he understands and knows me, that I am the Lord who practices steadfast love, justice, and righteousness in the earth. For in these things I delight, declares the Lord."

How can we know this transcendent God? The only way is for him to reveal himself to us. He reveals his existence and power in creation (see Psalm 19 and Romans 1:18-21). However, if we want to truly know the God who practices steadfast love, justice, and righteousness, it must be through the Word of God. This is why we study the Bible; it is God's revelation of himself to us. Second Peter 1:20-21 explains, "no prophecy of Scripture comes from someone's own interpretation. For no prophecy was ever produced by the will of man, but men spoke from God as they were carried along by the Holy Spirit." Hebrews 1:1-3 describes God speaking to people:

> Long ago, at many times and in many ways, God spoke to our fathers by the prophets, but in these last days he has spoken to us by his Son, whom he appointed the heir of all things, through whom also he created the world. He is the radiance of the glory of God and the exact imprint of his nature, and he upholds the universe by the word of his power….

This Son is Jesus Christ, the Word of God in flesh. Jesus said, "I am the way, and the truth, and the life. No one comes to the Father except through me. If you had known me, you would have known my Father also. From now on you do know him and have seen him" (John 14:6-7). So in a way, the teacher mentioned at the beginning was wrong. People have seen God. They have walked and talked with him. These eyewitnesses have written down their testimonies for us to read today. All of Scripture reveals God to us through his Son, Jesus (see John 5:39, Luke 24:25-27, 44).

So why study the Bible? Because we need to know who God truly is and guard against trying to paint our own fanciful picture of him. God has revealed himself to us not in paintings but through his Son by the words of the Scripture. God, the creator, has spoken, and we, his creation, should listen to his words as truth to our ears and rejoice. That is why we study the Bible—because it is the only way to truly know God.

The Bible study booklet you are holding is to assist you in studying Paul's letter to the Philippian Church in an **inductive** way. Inductive study happens when we read the passage in context and ask ourselves questions about the text with the purpose of deriving the meaning and significance from the text itself. We really do this every day with everything we read without realizing it. What we are after when we study the Bible inductively is the author's original intent; i.e., what the author meant when he wrote the passage. We figure out the meaning by asking a series of questions of the text, paying close attention to the words and context to answer those questions.

The benefit of inductive study is that we learn how to study the Bible on our own—a tool which can serve us well every day of our lives as we grow in our relationship with God. We can discover for ourselves the depth of the riches of Scripture, thus remembering it better and applying it more directly to our lives.

The theme of the letter to the Philippians is joy. May the Lord bring joy to your heart as you dig deeply in the Word of God.

How to Do Inductive Bible Study

Step 1 – Begin with prayer. "Open my eyes, that I may behold wondrous things out of your law" (Psalm 119:18).

Step 2 – Read the text.

Step 3 – Observation. *The goal of this step is to figure out what the text is saying.* This is where you ask questions like: Who? When? Where? What? These questions should be answered from the very words of the text. Ask yourself if this passage reminds you of any other passages in Scripture. Write down any questions that arise in your mind.

Step 4 – Interpretation. *The goal of this step is to figure out what the text meant to the original hearers.* This most important step is often skipped, but a lack of correct interpretation leads to incorrect application. We cannot understand what God is saying to us if we don't first understand what he was saying to his original audience, and why he was saying it.

Your job in interpretation is to figure out the main point of the passage and understand the arguments that support the main point. Your interpretation should flow out of your observations, so keep asking yourself, "Can I support this interpretation based on my observations?"

Following are some questions to ask yourself as you study:

- How does the surrounding context of the passage shed light on its meaning?

- Why did the author include this particular passage in his book?
- Do other passages of Scripture fill out my interpretation?
- Is my interpretation consistent with my overall observations or is it too dependent on a few details?
- How does this passage fit within the Bible's teaching as a whole? (The context of any passage is ultimately the Bible as a whole.)
- What is the main point of the passage?
- Can I summarize the passage in a few sentences?
- If an Old Testament passage: How does this passage relate to Christ and his work on the cross?

Step 5 – Application. *Prayerfully apply the passage to your own life.* The application should flow from the main point of the text.

Following are some questions to ask yourself in order to apply the text:

- Did I learn something new about God, his ways, his character, his plans, and his priorities? If so, how should I be living in light of this truth?
- Do I need to change my beliefs based on this passage, or is a truth reinforced?
- Is there a behavior I need to adopt or stop?
- Does this passage have implications for the way I should relate to the church?
- Does this passage have implications for the way I relate to or speak to my non-Christian friends?
- How should I pray based on this passage?
- Should I be praising God for something in this passage?
- Do I see a sin for which I need to repent?
- Is there an encouragement or promise on which I need to dwell?

In Summary

Luke 24:44-47 says,

Then [Jesus] said to them, "These are my words that I spoke to you while I was still with you, that everything written about me in the Law of Moses and the Prophets and the Psalms must be fulfilled." Then he opened their minds to understand the Scriptures, and said to them, "Thus it is written, that the Christ should suffer and on the third day rise from the dead, and that repentance and forgiveness of sins should be proclaimed in his name to all nations, beginning from Jerusalem."

This is why we study the Bible: so that we can know Christ, repent, be forgiven, and proclaim him to the nations. We must keep Jesus in mind when we study Scripture. Adrienne Lawrence writes, "God has one overarching redemptive plan—to glorify himself by creating and redeeming a people for himself through Christ. Christ is at the center of God's plan. All of Scripture in some way speaks to that plan. Keep this in mind as you are doing your study of Scripture."

[*Note: This "How to" has been adapted from Adrienne Lawrence's pamphlet on Inductive Bible Study.*]

Notes

The first day of this inductive study will be an overview of the letter to the Philippians. On the following days you will study smaller segments of the letter and answer observation, interpretation, and application questions. The questions were written based on language from the English Standard Version of the Bible. However, you are welcome to use any reliable translation to do the study.

To assist you in recognizing the different types of questions asked, the questions are set out with icons as indicated below.

👁 **Observation:** Look closely in order to figure out what the text is saying. Get answers directly from the text, using the words of Scripture.

✦ **Interpretation:** What's the "true north" for his verse? Figure out what the text meant to the original hearers by determining the author's intended meaning.

♥ **Application:** Apply the passage to your own heart and life, concentrating on the author's intended meaning that you have already determined.

Because Scripture interprets Scripture, many of the questions cite passages in addition to the one you are studying in Philippians. If the question says, "Read…" you will need to read the additional verses cited to answer the question. If the question says, "See…" the verses help you answer the question but are not necessary. "See also…" signals you to read the verses if you would like to study the answer to the question further.

You only need your Bible to do this study of Paul's letter to the Philippians, and, in fact, I highly recommend first answering the questions directly from your Bible before looking at any other materials. That said, it may be helpful for you to confirm your answers, especially if you are leading others in a group study. To check your answers or for further study, Don Carson's *Basics for Believers: An Exposition on Philippians*, is excellent. Alec Motyer has written a more detailed commentary, *The Message of Philippians*, that is also helpful.

For more general help in knowing how to study the Bible, I highly recommend *Bible Study: Following the Ways of the Word*, by Kathleen Buswell Nielson and *Dig Deeper! Tools to Unearth the Bible's Treasure*, by Nigel Beynon and Andrew Sach. Bible study teachers and students who want a closer look at New Testament theology that will also encourage your heart can read Thomas Schreiner's, *Magnifying God in Christ: A Summary of New Testament Theology*.

Notes for Leaders

This Bible study can be done by individuals alone, but the best context for Bible study is in the local church. When small groups of women gather together to study the Scriptures, it promotes unity and ignites spiritual growth within the church.

The study was designed for ladies to complete five days of "homework," and then come together to discuss their answers in a small group. The goal of gathering in small groups is to promote discussion among ladies to sharpen one another by making sure all understand the meaning of the text and can apply it to their lives. As ladies discuss, their eyes may be opened to applications of the text they didn't see while doing the individual study. Believers will encourage one another in their knowledge of the gospel, and unbelievers will hear the gospel clearly explained. As a result, ladies will learn from one another and come away from group Bible study with a deeper understanding of the text and a better knowledge of how to read the Bible on their own in their private times of study and prayer.

If you are leading a small group, you will have some extra homework to do. First, know what Bible study is and is not. Bible study is not primarily a place to meet felt needs, eat good food and chat, receive counseling or have a free-for-all discussion. All of these things tend to happen in a ladies' Bible study, but they should not take over the focus. Bible study is digging into the Scriptures to get the true meaning of the text and applying it to lives that change as a result.

Second, make sure you know the main points of the text before leading discussion by carefully studying the passage and checking yourself using a good commentary, like one of those listed above. You may also find a Bible dictionary and concordance helpful. Second Timothy 3:16-17 says, "All Scripture is breathed out by God and profitable for teaching, for reproof, for correction, and for training in righteousness, that the man [or woman] of God may be competent, equipped for every good work." Scripture is powerful. That power comes through truth. Scripture is not like a magical incantation: We say the words and see the effect. We must know what the text of Scripture means before we apply it and see its work of transformation in our lives. Your job as a discussion leader is not to directly teach, nor to simply facilitate discussion, but rather to lead ladies in finding the meaning of the text and help them see how it is "profitable" and can make them "competent, equipped for every good work."

Third, pray. Pray for the ladies in your group during the week while you prepare. Pray as you start your small group study, asking the Holy Spirit to illuminate the Scripture to your minds and apply it to your hearts. And encourage ladies to pray based on what they studied at the end of your small group time. Ask the Holy Sprit to use his sword, the Word of God, in the lives of your ladies.

Fourth, draw ladies out and keep your discussion organized. Choose what you determine are the most important questions from the study guide, focusing the bulk of your discussion on the interpretation and application questions. Ask a question, but don't answer it! Be comfortable with long pauses or rephrase questions you think the group didn't understand. Not answering the questions yourself may be a bit awkward at first, but it will promote discussion in the end because your ladies will know they have to do the answering. Feel free to affirm good answers or sum up after ladies have had time to discuss. This gives clarity to the discussion. However, don't feel the need to fill in every detail and nuance you gleaned from your personal study. Your goal is to get your group talking.

Fifth, keep your focus on the Scriptures. The Holy Spirit uses them to change ladies' hearts. Don't be afraid of wrong answers. Gently use them to clarify and teach by directing attention back to the Scriptures for the right answer. If ladies go off on unhelpful tangents, direct them back to the question and address the tangent later one on one or with reading material. However, if the tangent is on a vital question that goes to the gospel, take time to talk about it. These are God-given opportunities.

Sixth, be sure you focus on the gospel. In your prep time, be sure to ask yourself what the text has to do with the gospel and look for opportunities to ask questions to bring out the gospel. Hopefully, your church members will invite unbelievers to your study who will hear the glorious good news. But, even if your group is made up of all believers, we never get beyond our need to be reminded of Christ crucified and what that means for our lives.

Lastly, enjoy studying the Scriptures with your ladies. Your love for the Word of God will be contagious, and you will have the great joy of watching your ladies catch it and rejoice in the Word with you.

Paul and the Church at Philippi

Paul identifies himself as the author of the letter to the Philippians. Paul was an apostle, which means he was an eyewitness of Jesus and was specially sent of Christ. You can read in Acts about how Paul (then called Saul) met the risen Lord Jesus in an extraordinary way while he was traveling throughout the region of Palestine persecuting the church. (Acts 8:1-3 and 9:1-22) After Paul's conversion, he traveled widely in Asia and Europe, proclaiming the Gospel he had once tried to destroy and planting churches. Philippians is one of thirteen New Testament letters he wrote.

Paul planted the church at Philippi. After receiving a vision of a man urging him to come to Macedonia, Paul set sail to preach the Gospel in the city of Philippi in the district of Macedonia. After hearing Paul preach, the Lord opened the heart of a prominent woman of the city, Lydia, and she became the first Philippian convert. More conversions followed, even (or perhaps, especially) after Paul and his companion Silas were thrown in jail. By the time Paul and Silas left Philippi, there was a Philippian church. Read Acts 16:6-40 for the account of Paul's first visit to Philippi. Paul returned to the city to encourage the church on at least one more occasion. (Acts 20:1-6)

This first day we will do an overview of the entire letter. When the Philippian church received this letter from Paul it would have been read aloud to the entire congregation. They didn't have printing presses in the First Century, so a scribe would have to painstakingly copy every word. These letters were thus carefully preserved, and written copies would have been distributed to other churches to be read aloud to those congregations. Reading through the entire book in one sitting is valuable to us, not only because it gives us a feel for what happened in the First Century, but also because it gives us an overview of what the letter is about as we notice certain themes repeated throughout the letter.

Begin by praying, Lord *"Open my eyes, that I may behold wondrous things out of your law."* (Psalm 119:18)

Read through chapters 1–4 of the letter to the Philippians and do the following:

Write down any repeated words, phrases, or ideas you notice:

Jot down any questions that arise in your mind for later study:

Answer the following questions:

What are the circumstances in Paul's life when he writes the letter?

What is going on in the lives of the saints of Philippi (the church) when Paul writes the letter?

What is the overall tone of the letter?

Why did Paul write this letter to the church at Philippi?

Day 2

Remember:

- 👁 **Observation:** Figure out what the text is saying. Get the answer from the words of Scripture.
- ✛ **Interpretation:** Figure out the meaning of the text. What did the writer intend to convey?
- 💜 **Application:** Prayerfully apply the passage to your own life. The application should flow from the main point of the text.

Pray that you would know the grace and peace of God the Father and the Lord Jesus Christ.

Read Philippians 1:1-18.

Read verses 1-2.

👁 1. Who wrote this letter?

👁 2. What do Paul and Timothy call themselves?

💜 3. What does it mean to be "servants of Christ Jesus"?

✝ 4. Jesus had appeared in a vision and said, "[Paul] is a chosen instrument of mine to carry my name before the Gentiles and kings and the children of Israel" (Acts 9:15). Why would these church leaders call themselves servants instead of asserting their impressive credentials?

💜 5. What would be different in your interactions with others in your church if you thought of yourself, first and foremost, as a servant of Christ Jesus?

👁 6. To whom is the letter written?

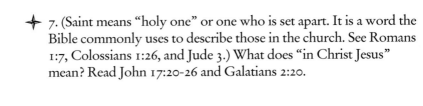 7. (Saint means "holy one" or one who is set apart. It is a word the Bible commonly uses to describe those in the church. See Romans 1:7, Colossians 1:26, and Jude 3.) What does "in Christ Jesus" mean? Read John 17:20-26 and Galatians 2:20.

✦ 8. Who are overseers? Read 1 Timothy 3:1-7.

✦ 9. Who are deacons? Read Acts 6:1-7 and 1 Timothy 3:8-13.

✦ 10. Why do you think this letter is written to saints in Philippi as well as to the overseers and deacons? (It could have been only written to the leaders of the church.)

♥ 11. Do the truths in this letter only apply to the saints, overseers, and deacons in the First Century church in Philippi, or can and should Christians apply these truths to our lives today? See 2 Timothy 3:16.

👁 12. How does Paul greet the church at Philippi?

👁 13. From where do grace and peace come?

✦ 14. Grace means a gift that is not earned or deserved (see Romans 11:5-6). Peace occurs when two or more parties are reconciled to one another. What do you think it means for grace and peace to come from "God our Father and the Lord Jesus Christ"?

✦ 15. Why do you think Paul opens his letter with this greeting?

♥ 16. Have you received grace and peace from God the Father and the Lord Jesus Christ? If so, what difference has it made in your life? If not, go back to the verses that explain what "in Christ Jesus" means and think through what it would mean in your life to accept grace and peace from God.

Pray that God would make you like a tree planted by streams of water—that your delight would be rooted in his law (Psalm 1:2-3).

Read Philippians 1:1-18.

Read verses 3-5.

👁 1. Having greeted the Philippians, how does Paul begin the rest of his letter?

👁 2. What is Paul thanking God for?

👁 3. How does Paul feel when he prays for the Philippian church?

👁 4. Why is Paul thankful for them?

👁 5. How is the Philippian church in partnership with Paul?

👁 6. How long has the Philippian church been in partnership with Paul?

✛ 7. What does it mean to be in "partnership in the gospel"? See Romans 10:12-15 and 1 Peter 2:9.

♥ 8. If you are a follower of Christ, describe the ways you partner with others in the gospel:

♥ 9. List some other ways you can partner with saints in your church in the gospel:

Day 4

Pray that God, who begins and completes his work in our hearts, will use this Bible study to work in your heart.

Read Philippians 1:1-11.

Read verse 6.

👁 1. Of what is Paul sure?

👁 2. To whom does the word *he* refer?

👁 3. What did God begin?

👁 4. What will God do?

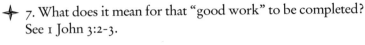 5. When will God bring his work to completion?

6. What is the "good work" that God began? See Ephesians 2:4-6.

7. What does it mean for that "good work" to be completed? See 1 John 3:2-3.

8. Who is beginning, bringing along, and completing the "good work?" See also 1 Thessalonians 5:23-24.

9. What is "the day of Jesus Christ"? Read 2 Thessalonians 1:7b-10.

10. What does verse 6 mean? Write it in your own words:

Week 1

♥ 11. Do you ever despair over your own sin? Do you ever feel far from God? If you are a saint in Christ Jesus considering this verse, how should you handle these times and emotions?

Read verses 7-8.

👁 12. What feeling is right for Paul?

👁 13. Where does Paul hold the Philippians?

👁 14. Why does Paul hold the Philippians in his heart?

👁 15. How are the Philippians partakers of grace with Paul?

👁 16. How much does Paul yearn for the Philippians?

✟ 17. Why does Paul care so much for the Philippians?

♥ 18. The Greek noun rendered "affection" in English was used often of Jesus in the Gospels and indicates deep emotion. Paul writes of his joy in relationship with and having this affection for the saints at Philippi. What can you do to have more relationships like this in your church?

♥ 19. Pray for the Lord to increase your partnership in the gospel, your affection for sisters and brothers in Christ, and joy in relationships with others in the church.

Day 5

Pray that your love would abound more and more with knowledge and all discernment as you study the Scriptures.

Read Philippians 1:1-11.

Read verse 9.

👁 1. What is Paul's prayer for the Philippians?

👁 2. With what does Paul pray for the Philippians' love to abound?

✦ 3. For whom is this love?

✦ 4. What kind of knowledge is Paul writing about?

✦ 5. What do these verses tell you about the kind of knowledge about which Paul is writing: Jeremiah 9:23-24, John 17:3, Galatians 4:8-9, Colossians 1:9-10, 2 Timothy 1:12.

✦ 6. What is discernment? See Romans 12:2 and Hebrews 4:12-13 and 5:14.

♥ 7. How can you fuel your love to abound more and more in knowledge and discernment?

Read verse 10a.

👁 8. What will result from the Philippians' love abounding with knowledge and all discernment?

✦ 9. What does it mean to "approve what is excellent"?

✦ 10. How does knowledge and discernment affect one's ability to approve what is excellent?

❤ 11. How would your life change if you only approved what is excellent? Consider the following things in your life...

    ❤ Movies/TV/music:

    ❤ Clothing:

♥ Speech/conversations:

♥ Reading/hobbies/activities:

♥ Use of time and money:

♥ 12. Can you think of any other areas in your life where you need to approve what is excellent?

Read verses 10b-11.

👁 13. What is the ultimate goal of the Philippians' love abounding with knowledge and discernment?

👁 14. Through whom does the fruit of righteousness come?

👁 15. What is the point of being pure, blameless, and filled with the fruit of righteousness?

✦ 16. What is the "day of Christ"? (It is also mentioned in verse 6. In addition, read Revelation 19:6-9.)

✦ 17. What is the "fruit of righteousness"? See Galatians 5:22-24.

✦ 18. How would you sum up Paul's prayer in verses 9-11 in your own words?

💗 19. Out of his great love for the saints of Philippi, Paul prays these God-honoring, powerful prayers of thanksgiving and supplication in verses 3-11. His prayers are targeted to encourage and build up the church. Examine the focus of your prayer life. How do you tend to pray for yourself and others? Use Paul's prayers to shift your prayer focus from temporal desires to spiritual needs. Think through how you can pray for the saints in your church to have love that abounds more and more in knowledge and all discernment.

Joy in the Advance of the Gospel

Day 1 - Review

Pray that the Lord will make known to you the path of life and that he will fill you with joy in his presence, with eternal pleasures at his right hand. Psalm 16:11.

Begin the week by reading through Philippians chapter 1.

Review your notes from week 1.

✦ 1. Remind yourself of the main points of Philippians 1:1-11 and jot them down:

♥ 2. After studying the first 11 verses of Philippians, how should your prayer life be affected?

♥ 3. What relationships in the church can you focus on to increase your partnership in the gospel? What do you need to do to make sure that these relationships are characterized by affection and joy?

♥ 4. Spend some time in prayer about your relationships in the church and the focus of your prayer life.

Day 2

Pray that the gospel would be the center of your life.

Read Philippians 1:12-18.

These verses focus on advancing the gospel and preaching Christ. Those are really two ways of saying the same thing. We cannot understand the letter to the Philippians unless we clearly understand what the gospel of Christ is. By the way, *gospel* is simply another way of saying, "good news." Today you will look at a number of verses in Scripture to make sure you know and can tell others the best news ever known to mankind.

Basically, the gospel has four components: God, Man, Christ, Response. Read the verses below in each of those categories, and then come up with a definition of the gospel in your own words.

God

God's Character Is Holy

Revelation 4:8 And the four living creatures, each of them with six wings, are full of eyes all around and within, and day and night they never cease to say, "Holy, holy, holy, is the Lord God Almighty, who was and is and is to come!"

Isaiah 6:1-5 In the year that King Uzziah died I saw the Lord sitting upon a throne, high and lifted up; and the train of his robe filled the temple. Above him stood the seraphim. Each had six wings: with two he covered his face, and with two he covered his feet, and with two he flew. And one called to another and said: "Holy, holy, holy is the LORD of hosts; the whole earth is full of his glory!" And the foundations of the thresholds shook at the voice of him who called, and the house was filled with smoke. And I said: "Woe is me! For I am lost; for I am a man of unclean lips, and I dwell in the midst of a people of unclean lips; for my eyes have seen the King, the LORD of hosts!"

God is the Creator
Genesis 1:1 In the beginning, God created the heaven and the earth.
John 1:1 In the beginning was the Word, and the Word was with God, and the Word was God.

God is Loving
Exodus 34:6 The LORD passed before him and proclaimed, "The LORD, the LORD, a God merciful and gracious, slow to anger, and abounding in steadfast love and faithfulness, keeping steadfast love for thousands, forgiving iniquity and transgression and sin, but who will by no means clear the guilty...
1 John 4:10 In this is love, not that we have loved God but that he loved us and sent his Son to be the propitiation for our sins.

Man

Humanity Is Created by God
Genesis 1:27 So God created man in his own image, in the image of God he created him; male and female he created them.

Humanity Is Sinful
Romans 3:23 ...for all have sinned and fall short of the glory of God.
Isaiah 53:6 All we like sheep have gone astray; we have turned— every one—to his own way; and the LORD has laid on him the iniquity of us all.

Humanity Is Headed for Death
Romans 6:23 For the wages of sin is death, but the free gift of God is eternal life in Christ Jesus our Lord.

Humanity Is Separated from God

Isaiah 59:2 But your iniquities have made a separation between you and your God, and your sins have hidden his face from you so that he does not hear.

Colossians 1:21 And you, who once were alienated and hostile in mind, doing evil deeds.

Jesus Christ

Jesus Is God in the Flesh

Luke 22:70 So they all said, "Are you the Son of God, then?" And he said to them, "You say that I am."

John 1:1-2 In the beginning was the Word, and the Word was with God, and the Word was God. He was in the beginning with God.

Jesus Lived a Sinless Life on Earth

2 Corinthians 5:21 For our sake he made him to be sin who knew no sin, so that in him we might become the righteousness of God.

1 Peter 2:22 He committed no sin, neither was deceit found in his mouth.

Jesus Reconciles Us to God

2 Corinthians 5:18-19 All this is from God, who through Christ reconciled us to himself and gave us the ministry of reconciliation; that is, in Christ God was reconciling the world to himself, not counting their trespasses against them, and entrusting to us the message of reconciliation.

Jesus Died in Our Place

Romans 5:8 But God shows his love for us in that while we were still sinners, Christ died for us.

Jesus Rose from the Dead

Acts 17:31 Because he has fixed a day on which he will judge the world in righteousness by a man whom he has appointed; and of this he has given assurance to all by raising him from the dead.

Jesus Is the Way to Eternal Life

John 3:16 For God so loved the world, that he gave his only Son, that whoever believes in him should not perish but have eternal life.
John 5:24 Truly, truly, I say to you, whoever hears my word and believes him who sent me has eternal life. He does not come into judgment, but has passed from death to life.

Response

Repent

To repent is to have an understanding of what the wrong is, a regret over what our selfishness results in, and a resolve to become what we were meant to be by God's grace. Repentance indicates willingness to change. But if it stops here, only a good resolution has been made.

Acts 2:38 And Peter said to them, "Repent and be baptized every one of you in the name of Jesus Christ for the forgiveness of your sins, and you will receive the gift of the Holy Spirit."
Acts 17:30 The times of ignorance God overlooked, but now he commands all people everywhere to repent.

Believe

Belief involves our mind, but in the true biblical sense, true belief or faith must lead to an action. Formal belief becomes real at the point that we act upon it.

John 3:18 Whoever believes in him is not condemned, but whoever does not believe is condemned already, because he has not believed in the name of the only Son of God.
John 5:24 Truly, truly, I say to you, whoever hears my word and believes him who sent me has eternal life. He does not come into judgment, but has passed from death to life.

[The above is based on a gospel summary written for Intervarsity Fellowship.]

✦ 1. Now, see if you can write the gospel in your own words. Imagine that you are explaining it to a friend. Don't forget the four components: God, Man, Christ, Response.

Day 3

Remember:

- 👁 **Observation:** Figure out what the text is saying. Get the answer from the words of Scripture.
- ✦ **Interpretation:** Figure out the meaning of the text. What did the writer intend to convey?
- 💜 **Application:** Prayerfully apply the passage to your own life. The application should flow from the main point of the text.

Pray that the Lord would open your lips for your mouth to declare his praise. Psalm 51:15.

Read Philippians 1:12-18.

Read verses 12-14.

👁 1. What does Paul want the Philippian church to know?

👁 2. What are the two ways that Paul's imprisonment has served to advance the gospel?

✦ 3. From where is Paul writing?

✦ 4. Why does Paul want his Philippian brothers and sisters to know that his imprisonment has served to advance the gospel?

✦ 5. What is Paul's attitude about his imprisonment?

♥ 6. What can you do to be more like Paul: using every circumstance in life to advance the gospel, instead of only finding hope in a change of circumstances?

♥ 7. Can you think of a way you can use a current difficult circumstance or relationship in your life to advance the gospel?

Pray that your confidence would come from the Lord.

Read Philippians 1:12-18.

Read verse 14.

👁 1. In whom are the brothers confident?

👁 2. What has caused the brothers to become confident?

👁 3. What has resulted from the brothers' confidence in the Lord?

✦ 4. What does it mean to be "confident in the Lord"?

✦ 5. Why would Paul's imprisonment cause others to be more confident in the Lord?

♥ 6. Paul was imprisoned for Christ and kept proclaiming Christ to his captors, so much so that the whole imperial guard and more knew about Christ. Are you so confident in the Lord in the midst of suffering that everyone around you knows it? How would your friends and family describe your attitude toward suffering?

✦ 7. Why would Paul's imprisonment result in others being even more bold and less fearful about telling the gospel? Why doesn't it do the opposite, causing others to clam up for fear they would also be imprisoned?

♥ 8. Consider what in your life is valuable enough for you to risk imprisonment. If you are a follower of Jesus, are you willing to risk everything for Christ—to speak the word? If so, how are you living in a way that is risky for Christ?

♥ 9. Are you bold to speak the word without fear? If not, examine your heart. What are you fearful of losing: your reputation, your physical well-being, your comfortable relationships with family and friends, your convenient lifestyle, your valuable time?

Pray that God would create in you a pure heart and renew a steadfast spirit within you. Psalm 51:10.

Read Philippians 1:12-18.

Read verses 15-18.

👁 1. From what motivations do some preach Christ?

👁 2. From what motivation do others preach Christ?

👁 3. What further motivates those who preach Christ from good will?

👁 4. What do those who preach Christ from rivalry want to see happen to Paul?

👁 5. What is Paul's response to all who preach Christ, no matter what their motivation?

👁 6. How does Paul feel when Christ is proclaimed?

✦ 7. What does it mean to "preach Christ"?

         Week 2

✦ 8. Paul tells the Philippians in 2:1-5 to do nothing from rivalry or conceit. How can he rejoice that Christ is preached even when some are doing it insincerely out of envy and rivalry?

✦ 9. Read through the verses again. What really matters to Paul?

♥ 10. Do you know the gospel well enough to explain it clearly to others? If not, go back and review the gospel outline given on Day 2 (see 1 Peter 3:15.) Write down any questions you have about the gospel.

♥ 11. Paul rejoiced even when people were preaching the gospel so that his suffering would increase. Does the preaching of Christ cause you to rejoice? If you are a Christian, you were chosen to "proclaim the excellencies of him who called you out of darkness into his marvelous light" (1 Peter 2:9). How can you more fully center your life on proclaiming Christ?

♥ 12. Read Romans 10:9-17. If you live in or near a city, you probably come into contact with people, maybe even neighbors, who have never heard the gospel. God has placed you in that city for a purpose. What can you do to reach out to people who have never heard about Jesus?

♥ 13. If you are not a believer in Christ, think through why. Write down what you don't believe about God, man, Christ, response, or whatever else is holding you back.

Day 1 - Review

Pray that the advance of the gospel would cause you to rejoice.

Read Philippians 1.

Review your notes from week 2.

✦ 1. Why is the apostle Paul rejoicing, and why does he want the Philippians to know about it?

✦ 2. What does Paul's prayer for the Philippians in verses 3-11 have to do with his positive report on his imprisonment in verses 12-18?

♥ 3. What in the Christian faith really excites you? What gets your heart pumping and brings you joy—hearing about miracles, healings, signs from God? Or is it the pure gospel, and that proclaimed, that makes you rejoice? Think through how your focus in life is similar to and different from Paul's. Then pray for a heart like Paul's.

♥ 4. If you are not a follower of Christ, think about what excites you in life. How is that different than what Paul rejoices about, and how long will it last?

Day 2

Remember:

- 👁 **Observation:** Figure out what the text is saying. Get the answer from the words of Scripture.
- ✦ **Interpretation:** Figure out the meaning of the text. What did the writer intend to convey?
- ♥ **Application:** Prayerfully apply the passage to your own life. The application should flow from the main point of the text.

Pray that the God of hope would fill you with all joy and peace in believing, so that by the power of the Holy Spirit you may abound in hope. Romans 15:13.

Read Philippians 1:18-30.

Read verses 18-20.

👁 1. What does Paul say he is doing and will do in verse 18?

👁 2. For what reason does Paul say he will rejoice?

👁 3. What are the two agencies of deliverance Paul mentions?

👁 4. What is Paul's eager expectation and hope?

✦ 5. Considering these verses together, from what does Paul believe he'll be delivered?

✦ 6. How should the Philippians be praying for Paul?

✦ 7. What do these verses show Paul is most concerned with?

✦ 8. There are many ways that Paul can honor Christ in life. He has a fruitful ministry of sharing the gospel and discipling believers. But how can Paul honor Christ by death?

♥ 9. How do your reactions to suffering show that you are, or are not, most concerned with honoring Christ?

♥ 10. In light of Paul's focus on honoring Christ during times of grave danger and suffering, how should we be praying for ourselves and each other during times of suffering?

Day 3

Pray that Christ would be all to you so that you can say with Paul, "For to me to live is Christ, and to die is gain" (Philippians 1:21).

Read Philippians 1:18-30.

Read verses 21-23.

👁 1. What does Paul say "to live" is?

👁 2. What does Paul say "to die" is?

👁 3. What does it mean for Paul to "live in the flesh"?

👁 4. From verse 23, why does Paul consider death his gain?

👁 5. Which would Paul rather do: live or die?

✦ 6. What does Paul mean when he says "to live is Christ"?

✦ 7. What is the "fruitful labor" Paul refers to?

✦ 8. Why does Paul think to depart would be better?

❤ 9. Think about whether you can say: "For to me to live is Christ, and to die is gain?" Is the life part or the death part harder for you to say? Explain your answer.

❤ 10. How can thinking about our eternity being with Christ spur us on to fruitful labor now?

♥ 11. If you are not a follower of Jesus, what do you think happens when you die? After answering that question, is there anything worth giving your life for?

Day 4

Pray that your soul would pant for the Lord as the deer pants for streams of water. Psalm 42:1.

Read Philippians 1:18-30.

Read verses 24-26.

👁 1. For whom is it necessary for Paul to remain in the flesh?

👁 2. How does Paul want his remaining alive to affect the Philippians?

👁 3. Who does Paul say will get glory when he returns to the Philippians?

✦ 4. How does Paul expect his deliverance from prison to affect the Philippian church?

✦ 5. Why does Paul care more about what will benefit the Philippians than his own desires?

✦ 6. What is it about Paul's relationship with the Philippians that enables him to know that he will bring them great joy when he is with them again? Reread verses 5-7.

✦ 7. Why would Christ Jesus get the glory if Paul returned to the Philippians?

❤ 8. In what kind of fruitful labor in the church are you involved?

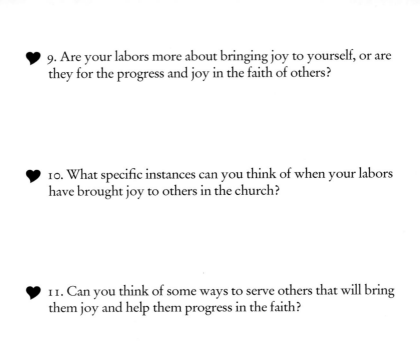

💜 9. Are your labors more about bringing joy to yourself, or are they for the progress and joy in the faith of others?

💜 10. What specific instances can you think of when your labors have brought joy to others in the church?

💜 11. Can you think of some ways to serve others that will bring them joy and help them progress in the faith?

Day 5

Pray that the Lord would show you his ways, teach you his paths, and guide you in his truth. Psalm 25:4.

Read Philippians 1:18-30.

Read verses 27-28.

👁 1. What manner of life does Paul exhort the Philippians to live?

👁 2. What will Paul hear of the Philippians if their manner of life is "worthy of the gospel"?

👁 3. What is a clear sign to the Philippians' opponents of their destruction and the Philippians' salvation?

👁 4. From whom is the Philippians' salvation?

✦ 5. What does it mean to stand "firm in one spirit, with one mind striving side by side for the faith of the gospel"?

✦ 6. According to these verses, is Christianity a religion that is lived out mainly in a personal, private way, or is it lived out in community with others? Explain.

❤ 7. In what ways do you live out your religion in a private way? In what ways do you strive side by side with others in the church for the gospel?

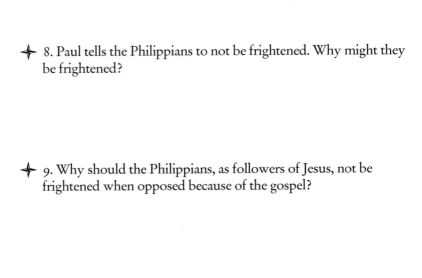

✦ 8. Paul tells the Philippians to not be frightened. Why might they be frightened?

✦ 9. Why should the Philippians, as followers of Jesus, not be frightened when opposed because of the gospel?

✦ 10. What is the destruction Paul writes about? Read 2 Thessalonians 1:5-12.

✦ 11. What is the salvation Paul writes about? Read 2 Thessalonians 1:5-12.

✦ 12. How does Paul's statement about "their destruction" and the Philippians' "salvation" encourage the Philippians to endure suffering?

♥ 13. How does thinking about your salvation and the destruction of those who oppose God encourage you to endure suffering for Christ?

Read verses 29-30.

👁 14. What has been granted to the Philippians?

👁 15. For whose sake have these things been granted?

👁 16. Who has had and is having the same conflict as the Philippians?

✦ 17. What does "granted" mean?

✦ 18. Who is the grantor?

✦ 19. Why has belief been granted to the Philippians? Read Ephesians 2:10 and 1 Peter 2:9.

✦ 20. If belief (or faith) is a gift, who gets the glory or credit for it?

✦ 21. How can suffering for the sake of Christ be a gift? Consider the previous verses from 12 on. Read also Matthew 5:10-12 and James 1:2-4.

✦ 22. How is Paul an example to the Philippians in times of conflict?

♥ 23. How does it affect your life to know that God grants belief in him as a gift?

   ♥ How does it change your motivations in life?

♥ How does it change the way you pray for others to come to know God?

♥ How does it change the way you share the gospel with others?

♥ 24. Have you ever suffered for the sake of Christ? Describe:

♥ How does seeing suffering for Christ as a gift change your attitude when you are going through that suffering?

♥ How does it change how you counsel others when they are suffering?

♥ How does it affect your prayers for yourself or others during times of suffering?

Philippians 2:1-11

Joy in Humility and Exaltation

Day 1 - Review

Pray that your eyes would be fixed on all of God's commandments, and your ways would be steadfast in keeping his statutes. Psalm 119:5-6.

Read Philippians 1.

Review your notes from week 3.

✦ 1. What are some of the main points of Philippians 1:18-30? (Pay special attention to your answers to the interpretation questions from week 3.)

♥ 2. How will you apply the meaning of these verses to your heart and life?

Remember:

- 👁 **Observation:** Figure out what the text is saying. Get the answer from the words of Scripture.
- ✦ **Interpretation:** Figure out the meaning of the text. What did the writer intend to convey?
- ♥ **Application:** Prayerfully apply the passage to your own life. The application should flow from the main point of the text.

Pray for your heart to be receptive to God's Word.

Read Philippians 1:27-2:18.

Read verses 2:1-4.

✦ 1. What does the "So" in the first verse refer back to?

👁 2. What are the four benefits in Christ that Paul mentions in v 1?

👁 3. What does Paul tell the Philippians to do if they have received these benefits?

👁 4. How does Paul further explain the meaning of "being of the same mind, having the same love, being in full accord and of one mind" in verses 3 and 4?

👁 5. What is it acceptable to do from rivalry or conceit?

👁 6. What is a humble attitude toward others?

👁 7. About whose interest should the Philippians be concerned?

✦ 8. What is the encouragement, comfort, love, participation in the Spirit, affection and sympathy that Paul writes about? What is it based on, and who is it from?

✦ 9. About what relationships is Paul specifically concerned in these verses?

✦ 10. What does it mean for the Philippians to be "of the same mind"?

✦ 11. What does it mean for the Philippians to "have the same love"?

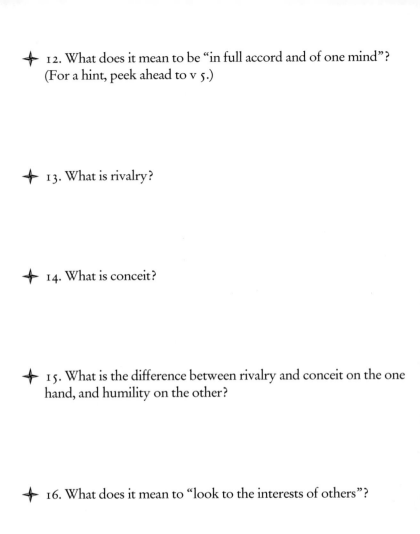

12. What does it mean to be "in full accord and of one mind"? (For a hint, peek ahead to v 5.)

13. What is rivalry?

14. What is conceit?

15. What is the difference between rivalry and conceit on the one hand, and humility on the other?

16. What does it mean to "look to the interests of others"?

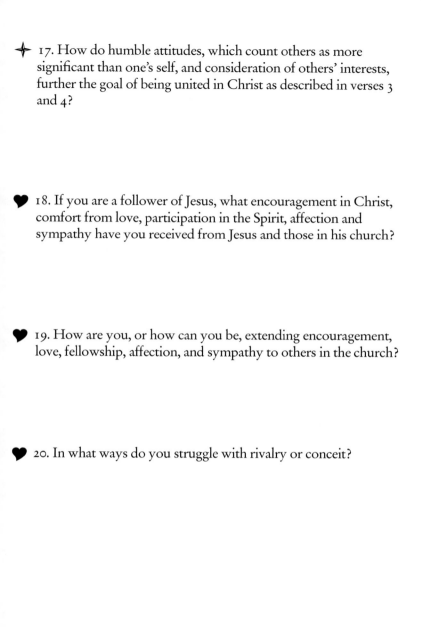

17. How do humble attitudes, which count others as more significant than one's self, and consideration of others' interests, further the goal of being united in Christ as described in verses 3 and 4?

18. If you are a follower of Jesus, what encouragement in Christ, comfort from love, participation in the Spirit, affection and sympathy have you received from Jesus and those in his church?

19. How are you, or how can you be, extending encouragement, love, fellowship, affection, and sympathy to others in the church?

20. In what ways do you struggle with rivalry or conceit?

♥ 21. Do you have a humble attitude? In what ways do you spend more time: thinking of your own interests or the interests of others? Explain.

♥ 22. How would your relationships in the church be different if your life was characterized by more humility?

♥ 23. How can you cultivate more humility in your life?

Day 3

Pray.

Read Philippians 2:1-11.

Read verses 5-8.

👁 1. What does Paul tell the Philippians to have?

✦ 2. To what kind of mind does the word "this" (in verse 5) refer?

👁 3. Paul tells the Philippians "this mind is yours." How is it theirs?

✦ 4. Why would Paul tell the Philippians to have "this mind" if it is already theirs in Christ Jesus?

👁 5. In whose form was Jesus?

👁 6. For what did Jesus not grasp?

👁 7. What did Jesus make himself?

👁 8. How did Jesus make himself nothing? What form did he take?

👁 9. In what likeness was Jesus born?

👁 10. How did Jesus humble himself?

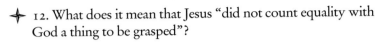 11. How obedient was Jesus?

✦ 12. What does it mean that Jesus "did not count equality with God a thing to be grasped"?

✦ 13. What did Jesus give up when he became man? Read John 17:5 and 2 Corinthians 8:9.

✦ 14. How was Jesus a servant?

✦ 15. In what ways was Jesus obedient? Read John 4:34 and Hebrews 4:15.

✦ 16. How was Jesus' death on the cross an act of obedience? Read Luke 22:41-44.

✦ 17. What do verses 6-8 imply about the relative importance of God and man? Was it a simple, comfortable thing for God to become man?

✦ 18. How does Jesus serve as the ultimate example of humility?

✦ 19. What does obedience have to do with humility?

♥ 20. How can you become more like Christ in obedience and humility?

✦ 21. Jesus serves as a perfect example for us, but he is also much more than just an example. Why did God send his Son to die on the cross? Read 1 Peter 3:18.

♥ 22. Dwell on the reality of God, the Creator of the Universe, sending his only Son into the world to die so that whoever believes in him will have eternal life. Praise God the Father for what he has done through his Son, Jesus.

Thou who wast rich beyond all splendour,
All for love's sake becamest poor;
Thrones for a manger didst surrender,
Sapphire-paved courts for stable floor.
Thou who wast rich beyond all splendour,
All for love's sake becamest poor.

Thou who art God beyond all praising,
All for love's sake becamest man;
Stooping so low, but sinners raising
Heavenwards by thine eternal plan.
Thou who art God beyond all praising,
All for love's sake becamest man.

Thou who art love beyond all telling,
Saviour and King, we worship thee.
Emmanuel, within us dwelling,
Make us what thou wouldst have us be.
Thou who art love beyond all telling,
Saviour and King, we worship thee.
　　　—Frank Houghton (1894–1972)

Pray.

Read Philippians 2:5-11.

✦ 1. What does it mean in verse 6 that Jesus was "in the form of God"? Read John 1:1-4, 14-18, and Colossians 1:15-20.

✦ 2. Did Jesus give up his divinity while he was on the earth, or did he remain fully God at all times? Read John 1:18, 5:18, 8:58-59, 10:30, and 20:28. Explain your answer.

✦ 3. Write what you learn about Jesus from each of these passages:

    ✦ John 1:1-3:

    ✦ John 5:18-24:

✦ Mark 1:9-11:

✦ Colossians 1:15-20:

♥ 4. Studying the verses above makes it even more amazing that Jesus took the form of a servant and gave himself up to die on a cross. What impact does this ultimate sacrifice have on your life?

Day 5

Pray.

Read Philippians 2:1-11.

Read verses 9-11.

👁 1. What has God done to Jesus?

👁 2. Why has God exalted Jesus? (Or what is the "Therefore" at the beginning of verse 9 there for?)

👁 3. What will every knee in heaven and on earth and under the earth do when the name of Jesus is mentioned?

👁 4. What will every tongue do?

👁 5. Who gets the glory when every knee bows and every tongue confesses Jesus Christ is Lord?

✛ 6. What does it mean that Jesus' name is "above every name"?

✛ 7. What does it mean for Jesus to be Lord? Reflect on Isaiah 45, especially verses 22-23.

✛ 8. How is it that every knee shall bow and every tongue confess that Jesus Christ is Lord?

✦ 9. When will that happen?

✦ 10. How does the acknowledgement of Jesus as Lord give God the Father glory?

♥ 11. Have you acknowledged Jesus as Lord? In what ways do you currently bow your knees and confess with your tongue that Jesus Christ is Lord?

♥ 12. Are there areas of your life in which you are resisting bowing your knees to Christ?

♥ 13. How should this truth that one day every knee will bow and every tongue confess Jesus Christ as Lord affect your relationships with those who don't currently confess Christ?

Philippians 2:12-30

Day 1 - Review

Pray.

Read Philippians 2:1-11.

Review your notes from week 4.

✦ 1. Why did Paul put a meditation on the humility and subsequent exaltation of Christ here in his letter to the Philippians?

✦ 2. Why is the unity of the saints in Philippi so important to Paul?

✦ 3. On what is the unity based?

✦ 4. What attitude and focus is needed to ensure unity in the church?

✦ 5. Who is clearly not only the head of the church but also the King of Kings?

♥ 6. How should Jesus' example of humility affect our lives? How should our lives be different in this area?

♥ 7. If we engage in rivalry, are conceited, or are more concerned about our interests than the interests of others, what does that say about whether we are bowing our knees and confessing with our tongues that Jesus Christ is Lord?

Day 2

Pray.

Read Philippians 2:1-18.

Read verses 12-13.

✦ 1. What is the "therefore" there for? To what is it pointing back?

2. What does Paul say the Philippians have always done?

3. What does Paul tell the Philippians to "work out"?

4. How are the Philippians to work it out?

5. Is salvation by works? Read Romans 3:21-28 and Ephesians 2:8-10 and Philippians 3:8-9. In light of these passages (and assuming Paul does not contradict himself), explain what you think it means to "work out your own salvation"?

6. What does the Philippians' obedience (as mentioned earlier in verse 12) have to do with working out their salvation?

7. What does Paul mean when he tells the Philippians to "work out their salvation with fear and trembling"?

✦ 8. Why is God someone who should be approached with fear and trembling? Read Deuteronomy 4:24, 5:23-26; Isaiah 6:1-5; and 1 Timothy 6:16. See also Daniel 10:4-9 and Revelation 4.

♥ 9. In your life, what is the evidence that you are serious about working out your salvation? Below are some questions to help you assess your spiritual life.

> ♥ What example can you give of obeying the Lord when it wasn't easy?

> ♥ How are you growing in the fruit of the Spirit? Read Galatians 5:22.

> ♥ What are examples of how you are fighting sin in your life, using the sword of the Spirit which is the Word of God? See Ephesians 6:17.

💜 How are you loving the saints? See 1 John 5:1.

💜 When is the last time you shared the gospel? See Matthew 28:19-20.

💜 Do you take time daily to know God better through his Word? See Luke 4:4.

💜 Do you take time daily to trust the Lord in prayer?

💜 10. Does your knowledge that God is to be approached with fear and trembling affect your reading of Scripture, prayer, and corporate gatherings on Sundays? How so?

Pray.

Read Philippians 2:12-18.

Read verse 13.

👁 1. Who works in the Philippians?

👁 2. In what two ways does God work in the Philippians?

👁 3. For whose pleasure do God and the Philippians work?

✦ 4. What does it mean for God to work "in you, both to will and to work"? (As you answer, distinguish between *to will* and *to work*.)

👁 5. Go back to verse 12: Who is Paul telling to work?

👁 6. But who is doing the work in verse 13?

Week 5

✦ 7. How can Paul tell the Philippians to work and at the same time write that God is doing the work? See 1 Corinthians 12:4-5, 15:10; Ephesians 2:10; Philippians 1:6 and Hebrews 13:20-21.

♥ 8. Don Carson writes:

> It is vitally important to grasp the connection between God's sovereignty and our responsibility in verses 12 and 13. The text does not say, "Work to acquire your salvation, for God has done his bit and now it is all up to you." Nor does it say, "You may already have your salvation, but now perseverance in it depends entirely on you." Still less does it say, "Let go and let God. Just relax. The Spirit will carry you." Rather, Paul tells us to work out our salvation with fear and trembling, precisely because God is working in us both to will and to act according to his good purpose (2:12-13)....God himself is working in us both to will and to act: he works in us at the level of our wills and at the level of our doing. (*Basics for Believers*, Baker Academic, 1996 pp. 61-62.)

♥ How is God's work in our lives an incentive for us to persevere and work for his good pleasure?

♥ If it is God who works in us both to will and to act, how should that impact the time we spend with the Lord in prayer?

Day 4

Pray.

Read Philippians 2:1-18.

Read verses 14-18.

👁 1. What does Paul tell the Philippians to do "without grumbling and questioning"?

👁 2. Why does he tell them not to grumble and question?

👁 3. What are the Philippians in the midst of?

👁 4. If the Philippians don't grumble and question, what will they be like among those of a crooked and twisted generation?

👁 5. What are the Philippians to hold fast to?

👁 6. If the Philippians hold fast to the word of life, when will Paul be proud?

👁 7. How does Paul feel about sacrificing for the sake of the Philippians' faith?

👁 8. How should the Philippians feel?

✦ 9. What does it mean to "grumble and question"? (Other translations read "complain or argue.")

✦ 10. Why do you think Paul would address grumbling and questioning here? (Think about the verses you studied last week.)

✦ 11. Who might the Philippians be grumbling against?

✦ 12. In Numbers 11:1-15, see how God dealt with the Israelites' grumbling against him and Moses after God had delivered them from Egypt. Why does God treat grumbling so seriously?

✦ 13. How can doing all things without grumbling and questioning make one "blameless and innocent"?

✦ 14. How would the Philippians "shine as lights in the world" by not grumbling and questioning?

✦ 15. What is the word of life?

✦ 16. What does "holding fast to the word of life" have to do with not grumbling and questioning?

✦ 17. When is the day of Christ?

✦ 18.What is Paul referring to when he writes of his running and laboring?

✦ 19. Why would Paul have the right to be proud of the Philippians?

✦ 20. What possibility is Paul alluding to in verse 17? See also 1 John 3:16.

✦ 21. Why would Paul rejoice even if his life is sacrificed? What is more important to Paul: his life or the Philippians' faith? Why?

✦ 22. Is Paul telling the Philippians that they should also rejoice in his suffering, their own suffering, or both? Why should they rejoice in suffering?

✦ 23. How are verses 14-18 related to "working out your own salvation with fear and trembling"?

♥ 24. Obviously, asking questions is not always wrong. Paul is writing against the questions that come from an argumentative, rebellious heart. As you answer this and the following questions, remember that your heart is the issue. Sometimes we don't complain out loud but grumble in our hearts.

♥ In what ways do you grumble against or question God?

♥ In what ways do you grumble against or question your church or its leaders?

♥ In what ways do you grumble against or question other followers of Jesus?

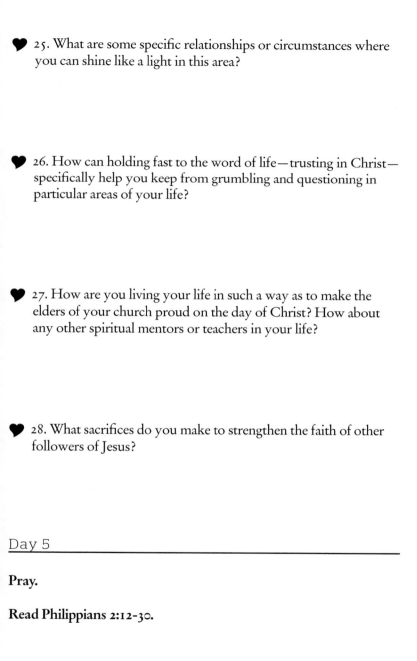

♥ 25. What are some specific relationships or circumstances where you can shine like a light in this area?

♥ 26. How can holding fast to the word of life—trusting in Christ—specifically help you keep from grumbling and questioning in particular areas of your life?

♥ 27. How are you living your life in such a way as to make the elders of your church proud on the day of Christ? How about any other spiritual mentors or teachers in your life?

♥ 28. What sacrifices do you make to strengthen the faith of other followers of Jesus?

Day 5

Pray.

Read Philippians 2:12-30.

Read verses 19-30.

👁 1. For what does Paul hope in verse 19?

👁 2. In whom does Paul hope?

👁 3. What does Paul hope to get from Timothy?

👁 4. What is Timothy genuinely concerned about?

👁 5. How does Paul describe Timothy?

👁 6. What kind of relationship does Paul have with Timothy?

👁 7. What does Paul trust will happen shortly?

👁 8. In whom does Paul trust?

👁 9. Whom else is Paul sending?

👁 10. Describe Paul's relationship with Epaphroditus.

👁 11. What had happened to Epaphroditus?

👁 12. How are the Philippians to receive Epaphroditus?

👁 13. Why should the Philippians honor Epaphroditus and others like him?

✦ 14. Paul "hope[s] in the Lord Jesus" and "trust[s] in the Lord" when he writes of the future. Why does he include these phrases? See James 4:13-16.

✦ 15. What relationship does Epaphroditus have with the Philippian church?

✦ 16. Describe in your own words Paul's relationship with Timothy and Epaphroditus.

✦ 17. How are Timothy and Epaphroditus similar?

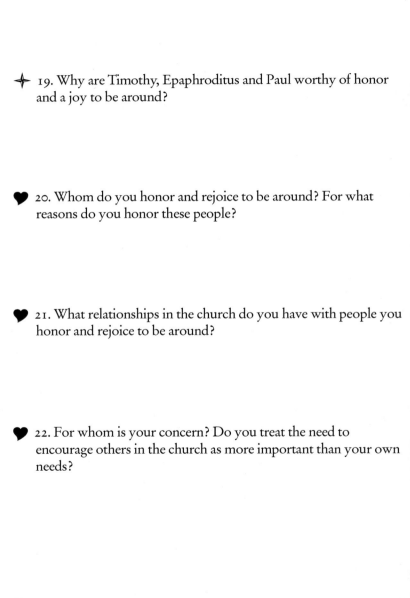

✦ 18. Who are Timothy and Epaphroditus concerned for?

✦ 19. Why are Timothy, Epaphroditus and Paul worthy of honor and a joy to be around?

♥ 20. Whom do you honor and rejoice to be around? For what reasons do you honor these people?

♥ 21. What relationships in the church do you have with people you honor and rejoice to be around?

♥ 22. For whom is your concern? Do you treat the need to encourage others in the church as more important than your own needs?

Pray.

Review your notes from week 5.

Read Philippians 2:12-30.

✦ 1. What is the focus of Paul's relationships with the Philippians and others, like Timothy and Epaphroditus?

♥ 2. What is the focus of your relationships, and why?

♥ 3. Can you say with Paul that you rejoice at sacrifices you make to strengthen the faith of other followers of Jesus? Give examples:

✦ 4. What verses or main points really stand out to you from last week's study?

♥ 5. How can you apply last week's verses to your life?

Day 2

Pray.

Read Philippians 3.

Read verses 1-6.

👁 1. What does Paul call the Philippians?

👁 2. What does Paul tell the Philippians to do in verse 1?

👁 3. What is no trouble to Paul and safe for the Philippians?

👁 4. For whom does Paul tell the Philippians to look out?

👁 5. How does Paul further describe who the dogs are?

👁 6. Who does Paul contrast the dogs with in verse 3?

👁 7. What three things do those who are the "real circumcision" do?

    👁 How do they worship?

    👁 In whom do they glory?

    👁 How much confidence do they put in the flesh?

👁 8. Why would Paul have reason for confidence in the flesh?

✦ 9. Why does Paul begin this section reminding the Philippians to rejoice?

✦ 10. In what way is Paul concerned about the safety of the Philippians?

✦ 11. What is circumcision? Read Genesis 17:9-14.

NOTE: Circumcision was the sign of inclusion into the covenant people of God—the nation of Israel—in the Old Testament. In the First Century when Paul wrote his letter, some argued that physical circumcision was still required for inclusion into the new covenant people of God—the church.

✦ 12. Look at the three things that distinguish those of the real circumcision: worshiping by the Spirit of God, glorying in Christ Jesus, and putting no confidence in the flesh. What is this circumcision that Paul is writing about? Read Deuteronomy 30:6, Romans 2:28-29 and Galatians 3:6-14.

✦ 13. What does "worship by the Spirit of God" mean? Read John 4:23-26.

✦ 14. What does it mean to "glory in Christ Jesus"? See 1 Corinthians 1:28-30.

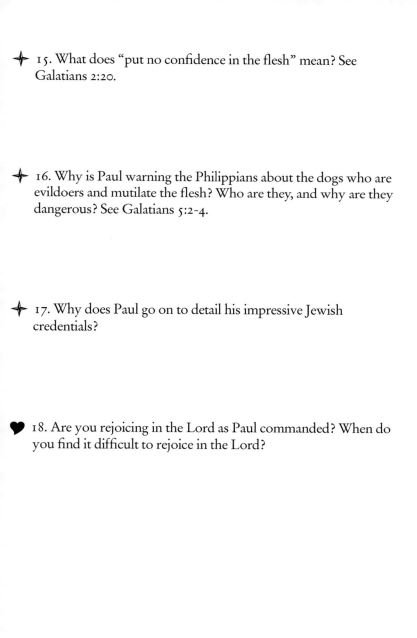

✦ 15. What does "put no confidence in the flesh" mean? See Galatians 2:20.

✦ 16. Why is Paul warning the Philippians about the dogs who are evildoers and mutilate the flesh? Who are they, and why are they dangerous? See Galatians 5:2-4.

✦ 17. Why does Paul go on to detail his impressive Jewish credentials?

♥ 18. Are you rejoicing in the Lord as Paul commanded? When do you find it difficult to rejoice in the Lord?

♥ 19. Are you part of the circumcision that Paul describes? Search your heart to answer the following questions:

♥ Do you worship by the Spirit of God? Explain.

♥ Do you glory only in Christ Jesus? How does your life show it?

♥ Do you put confidence in the flesh or trust in Christ alone for your salvation? How do you trust him for day to day living?

♥ 20. In what ways do you struggle with putting confidence in the flesh?

♥ 21. Do you watch out for dogs, evildoers and mutilaters of the flesh? How do you treat teaching that encourages confidence in the flesh, undermines the gospel, and threatens the safety of your soul?

Day 3

Pray.

Read Philippians 3:1-11.

Read verses 7-8.

✟ 1. Looking back at the previous verses, what gain is Paul talking about?

👁 2. For whose sake does Paul count these things as loss?

👁 3. What else does Paul count as loss?

👁 4. Why does Paul count everything as loss?

👁 5. What is of surpassing worth?

👁 6. Paul says that he has suffered the loss of all things. What does he call all those things toward the end of verse 8?

👁 7. Why has Paul suffered the loss of all things and counted them as rubbish? What does Paul want to gain?

✦ 8. What losses has Paul suffered? What does the "everything" and the "all things" refer to? See 2 Corinthians 11:21b-28.

✦ 9. What does "surpassing worth" mean?

✦ 10. Why does Paul consider knowing Christ Jesus to be worth more than anything else?

✦ 11. Why does Paul call all his learning, status, ability, and fleshly competence rubbish?

✦ 12. What does Paul believe is necessary to gain Christ?

♥ 13. What do you value more than knowing Christ? As you answer this question, consider what is reflected in your bank statement, weekly schedule, and use of free time.

♥ 14. What would your husband, children, and friends say if you asked them to tell you what they think is most important to you?

♥ 15. What will you do to cultivate a heart that considers everything as loss compared with the surpassing worth of knowing Christ Jesus?

Day 4

Pray.

Read Philippians 3:1-11.

Read verse 9.

1. In whom does Paul want to be found?

2. About what two kinds of righteousness does Paul write?

3. From where is the righteousness that comes through faith in Christ?

4. On what does that righteousness depend?

5. What is Paul referring to when he writes of the righteousness that comes from the law?

6. Explain the righteousness that comes through faith in Christ. Read Romans 3:21-26 and Ephesians 2:8-10.

7. What does it mean to be "found in [Christ]"? Read John 15:4-11.

✦ 8. Can a person be truly righteous apart from Christ? Read Romans 3:10-24. Explain your answer.

♥ 9. Search your heart. Have you received the righteousness from God that comes through faith in Jesus Christ? If you want the same joy and security in the midst of suffering that Paul has, it is only through Christ. Repent of your sin, and put your trust in him.

♥ 10. Pray for specific people you know who don't have faith in Christ. Also pray for people in North Africa and the Middle East who are trapped in Islam and have never heard the good news of Jesus Christ.

♥ 11. Pray that you will have a chance to share the good news of Jesus Christ with someone this week.

Pray.

Read Philippians 3.

Read verses 10-11.

👁 1. Who and what does Paul want to know?

👁 2. In what does Paul want to share?

👁 3. How does he want to become like Christ?

👁 4. What does Paul want to attain?

👁 5. By what means is he ready to attain it?

✦ 6. What does it mean to "know Christ"?

✦ 7. To what does the "power of his resurrection" refer? Read Colossians 1:11 and 2 Peter 1:3-4.

✦ 8. Why does Paul desire suffering? See 1 Peter 2:19-24, 4:1-2, 12-14.

✦ 9. What does "becoming like him in his death" mean? Read 2 Corinthians 4:6-11.

✦ 10. What does Paul want more than anything else? For what is he willing to suffer anything?

♥ 11. What do you want most in life? What is your deepest desire for yourself?

12. When you go through times of suffering do you desire most for God to change your circumstances, or do you want him to use them to make you more like him? What do you pray for during times of suffering: patience and endurance with joy, or "Get me out of this situation!"? Discuss.

Philippians 3:12-4:1

Day 1 - Review

Pray.

Review your notes from week 6.

Read Philippians 3:1-11.

✦ 1. What verses or main points stood out to you last week?

♥ 2. How can you apply the Scripture from last week to your life?

♥ 3. How would your life look different if you considered everything rubbish compared to the surpassing worth of knowing Christ? Consider your money, time, house, family, friendships, and church.

Pray.

Read Philippians 3-4:1.

Read verses 12-14.

✦ 1. What does the "this" in verse 12 refer to?

👁 2. Does Paul claim to be perfect?

👁 3. Instead of claiming to be perfect, what does Paul do?

✦ 4. What does the "it" in verse 12 refer to?

👁 5. To whom does Paul belong?

👁 6. What does Paul say he forgets?

👁 7. To what does Paul say he strains forward?

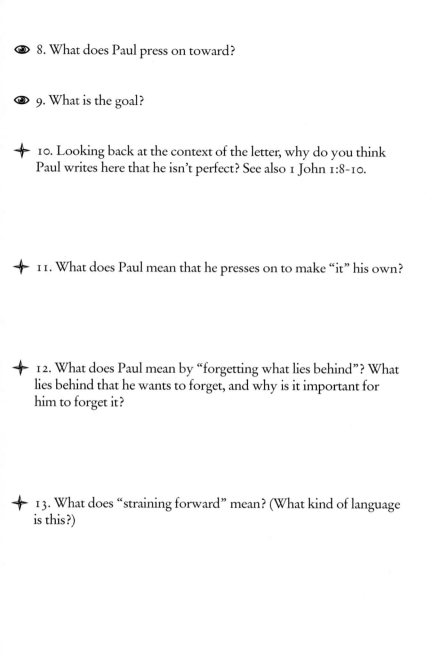

8. What does Paul press on toward?

9. What is the goal?

10. Looking back at the context of the letter, why do you think Paul writes here that he isn't perfect? See also 1 John 1:8-10.

11. What does Paul mean that he presses on to make "it" his own?

12. What does Paul mean by "forgetting what lies behind"? What lies behind that he wants to forget, and why is it important for him to forget it?

13. What does "straining forward" mean? (What kind of language is this?)

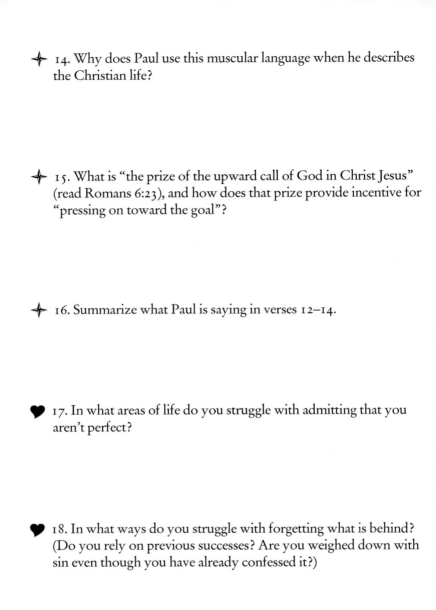

14. Why does Paul use this muscular language when he describes the Christian life?

15. What is "the prize of the upward call of God in Christ Jesus" (read Romans 6:23), and how does that prize provide incentive for "pressing on toward the goal"?

16. Summarize what Paul is saying in verses 12–14.

17. In what areas of life do you struggle with admitting that you aren't perfect?

18. In what ways do you struggle with forgetting what is behind? (Do you rely on previous successes? Are you weighed down with sin even though you have already confessed it?)

♥ 19. How does being made Christ's own and knowing the prize awaits you motivate you to press on? (Do you need to dwell more on these promises?)

♥ 20. If you were going to run a marathon or compete in a professional tennis tournament in six months, you would train every day rigorously. What are you doing to strain forward and press on toward the goal in your Christian life?

♥ 21. As Paul writes this letter, he has been a follower of Jesus for some 30 years and has suffered greatly for the gospel. He is an apostle who is writing Scripture—the very words of God, and he tells the churches to imitate him in the way he lives his life. How should Paul's confession that he is not perfect but presses on affect our lives?

Day 3

Pray.

Read Philippians 3:12-4:1.

Read verses 15-16.

👁 1. Who is supposed to "think this way"?

👁 2. What will happen to those who think otherwise?

👁 3. What does Paul urge the Philippians to do in verse 16?

✦ 4. What does "this way" refer to in verse 15?

✦ 5. Why did Paul write verse 15? What might some of the Philippians "think otherwise" about?

✦ 6. Who reveals the truth of Scripture?

✦ 7. Does Paul seem worried that some Philippians might not agree with him, or does he seem confident that God will reveal the truth of his position? Why?

✦ 8. What have the Philippians attained that Paul wants them to hold true to?

✦ 9. Why does Paul urge the Philippians to hold true to what they have attained, even if they don't totally agree with what Paul has written?

♥ 10. How can you make sure to hold true to what you have attained?

♥ 11. If you are a follower of Jesus, pray that you will hold onto the gospel . Also, pray that God will reveal the truth of Scripture to you as you study it, so "that your love may abound more and more, with knowledge and all discernment, so that you may approve what is excellent, and so be pure and blameless for the day of Christ, filled with the fruit of righteousness that comes through Jesus Christ, to the glory and praise of God" (Philippians 1:9-11).

Pray.

Read Philippians 3:12–21.

Read verses 17-19.

👁 1. What does Paul tell the Philippians to do in verse 17?

👁 2. Who has Paul warned the Philippians about?

👁 3. How does he feel as he warns the Philippians?

👁 4. How does Paul further describe enemies of the cross?

👁 5. What is their end?

👁 6. Who is their god?

👁 7. What do they glory in?

👁 8. What are their minds set on?

✦ 9. Paul has already admitted he is not perfect. Thinking back over what you have previously studied in Philippians, what makes Paul worthy of imitation?

✦ 10. How do those who walk according to the example the Philippians have in Paul and Timothy walk? What does this mean?

✦ 11. Why is Paul in tears as he is warning the Philippians of enemies of the cross?

✦ 12. What does it mean that these enemies' end is destruction?

✦ 13. What does "their god is their belly" mean?

✦ 14. What does "they glory in their shame" mean?

✦ 15. What does it mean to have "minds set on earthly things"?

✦ 16. Overall, how would you describe these enemies of the cross?

✦ 17. Compare the description of the enemies of the cross in verse 19 to the description of those who are the circumcision in verse 3. Sum up the differences.

♥ 18. Whom do you seek to imitate? Do you imitate Paul and others in the Scriptures? Are there other people who walk according to the example of Paul whom you imitate?

♥ 19. Are you able to say to younger Christians, "imitate me"? Are you walking according to the example of Paul, i.e. according to Scripture?

♥ 20. Do you weep over and for enemies of the cross? What should our attitudes be toward unbelievers?

♥ 21. When you look at the description of enemies of the cross, does it sound like you at all? Is your belly ever your god? (Do you think more of your physical comfort or your spiritual well-being?) Do you ever glory in what should be shameful to you? Is your mind often set on earthly things? Describe. (And then confess these things to God.)

Day 5

Pray.

Read Philippians 3:12-4:1.

Read verses 3:20-21.

👁 1. Where is the Philippians' citizenship?

👁 2. Who do the Philippians await?

👁 3. Who is the Philippians' Savior?

👁 4. What will Jesus do?

👁 5. By what power will Jesus transform our bodies?

👁 6. What things are subject to Christ?

✦ 7. What does it mean to have "citizenship in heaven"? Read Hebrews 11:13-16.

✦ 8. How is the Lord Jesus Christ the Savior? Read John 3:16-18 and Acts 4:11-12.

✦ 9. Why are the Philippians waiting for Jesus?

✦ 10. What does it mean that Jesus will "transform our lowly body to be like his glorious body"? Read 1 Corinthians 15:42-49.

✦ 11. What does this have to do with the previous verses, 12-14?

✦ 12. What power enables Jesus to transform bodies and subject all things to himself? Read Colossians 1:15-20.

♥ 13. Do you consider heaven your home? How would your daily life change if you were looking forward to going home to heaven?

♥ 14. If you are a follower of Jesus, have you dwelt on the fact that your body will be transformed to be glorious? How should that fact change the way you view sin in your life now?

♥ 15. How does it affect your life to know that all things are subjected to Jesus and that he will use that same power to transform your life?

Read verse 4:1.

👁 16. How does Paul feel about the Philippians?

👁 17. What are the Philippians to Paul?

👁 18. What does Paul tell the Philippians to do?

✦ 19. Why does Paul have such love for the Philippians?

✦ 20. How can he call them his joy and crown?

✦ 21. What does Paul mean by "stand firm in the Lord"?

✦ 22. Why does he urge the Philippians to stand firm at this point in the letter? (Think about what the "therefore" is there for.)

❤ 23. Do you love the church the way Paul does? How can you cultivate a greater love for your brothers and sisters in the church?

❤ 24. What work are you doing to build up the saints that gives you joy and earns you a crown?

❤ 25. What are you doing to ensure that you will stand firm in the Lord?

❤ 26. What role does your local church play in helping you to stand firm in the Lord?

Philippians 4:2-9

Day 1 - Review

Pray.

Review your notes from week 7.

Read Philippians 3:12-4:1.

💜 1. Many Christian authors and teachers claim to have simple answers or "secrets" that will make our lives easier or miraculously better. In light of these verses and the view of Christian life that Paul presents, should we be looking for quick fixes to the sin in our lives, or should we expect to work hard against sin by the power of the sword of the Spirit which is the Word of God? Explain.

✦ 2. What words or phrases in the passage tell you the Christian life is active work against sin?

💜 3. What motivates you to press on?

♥ 4. Do you know the Lord Jesus Christ as your Savior? Describe what he has saved you from and what he has saved you for.

Day 2

Pray.

Read Philippians 4.

Read verses 2-3.

👁 1. What does Paul entreat Euodia and Syntyche to do?

👁 2. The "true companion" is most likely a leader in the Philippian church to whom the letter was being delivered. What does Paul ask the true companion to do?

👁 3. How does Paul describe Euodia and Syntyche?

👁 4. Where are these ladies' names written?

✦ 5. How strongly does Paul feel about Euodia and Syntyche reconciling? What in the text shows Paul's strong feelings?

✦ 6. Why do you think Paul addresses, not only the ladies who are in conflict, but also a leader in the church (and really the whole church by putting it in the letter) when he writes urging reconciliation?

✦ 7. What does it mean that these women have their "names written in the book of life"? Read Revelation 20:11-15. See also Luke 10:20 and Revelation 3:5.

✦ 8. Why would Paul have written about the ladies' names being written in the book of life?

♥ 9. If we are followers of Jesus, how concerned should we be about conflict between sisters or brothers in our church?

♥ 10. Are you in conflict with anyone in your church? How can you go about reconciling?

Day 3

Pray.

Read Philippians 4:2-9.

Read verses 4-7.

👁 1. What does Paul command in verse 4?

👁 2. In what are the Philippians to rejoice?

👁 3. When are the Philippians to rejoice in the Lord?

👁 4. How long are the Philippians to rejoice in the Lord?

👁 5. What does Paul tell the Philippians to do in verse 5?

👁 6. What does Paul command at the beginning of verse 6?

👁 7. Why should the Philippians not be anxious? (See the phrase before the command.)

◉ 8. About what is it okay to be anxious?

◉ 9. What are the Philippians to do instead of being anxious?

◉ 10. With what are the Philippians' prayers to be infused?

◉ 11. What is the result of not being anxious but being thankful and presenting requests to God?

◉ 12. What guards hearts and minds in Christ Jesus?

✦ 13. We can tell several things from the letter to the Philippians: the church is undergoing some persecution (1:27-30); there are false teachers in their midst (3:2); and there is conflict among believers in the church (4:2-3). What do they have to rejoice about?

✦ 14. What does it mean to "let your reasonableness be known to everyone," and why would Paul write this here in his letter?

✦ 15. What does "The Lord is at hand" mean?

✦ 16. Why is the presence of the Lord the antidote for anxiety or fear? See Isaiah 41:10.

✦ 17. How does prayer acknowledge that God is near?

✦ 18. Why is thanksgiving so important in prayer?

✦ 19. Why should the Philippians make their request known to God? Doesn't he already know everything?

✦ 20. How does one experience the peace of God, and what is it like?

✦ 21. How does that peace surpass all understanding?

✦ 22. What does it mean to have "hearts and minds in Christ Jesus," and how does the peace of God guard hearts and minds in Christ Jesus?

✦ 23. What does rejoicing, reasonableness, the Lord being near, not being anxious, and prayer and thanksgiving have to do with the peace of God guarding hearts and minds in Christ Jesus? (Can you summarize verses 4-7?)

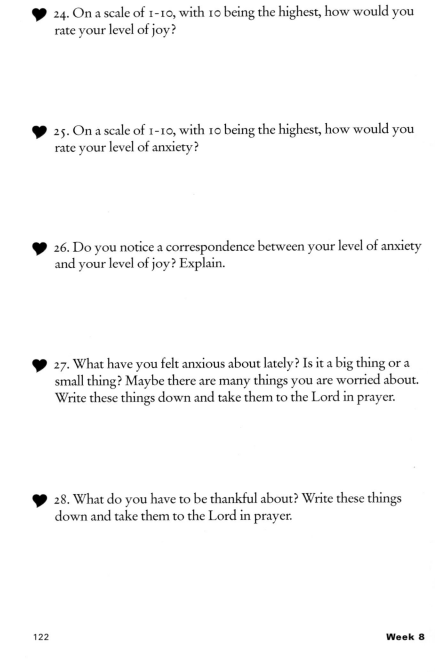

♥ 24. On a scale of 1-10, with 10 being the highest, how would you rate your level of joy?

♥ 25. On a scale of 1-10, with 10 being the highest, how would you rate your level of anxiety?

♥ 26. Do you notice a correspondence between your level of anxiety and your level of joy? Explain.

♥ 27. What have you felt anxious about lately? Is it a big thing or a small thing? Maybe there are many things you are worried about. Write these things down and take them to the Lord in prayer.

♥ 28. What do you have to be thankful about? Write these things down and take them to the Lord in prayer.

♥ 29. Are you known for being reasonable? In what circumstances or areas in life do you unreasonably demand (overtly or covertly) to have things your own way? (To answer this question, consider your emotional reactions to difficult circumstances.)

♥ 30. Do you live like the Lord is near? To think this through, consider these areas of your life: prayer, obedience, attitude, thoughts, hearing from God's Word.

♥ 31. Dwell on verses 4 to 7. How can your day-to-day life be different if you follow these commands?

Day 4

Pray.

Read Philippians 4:2-9.

Read verses 8-9.

👁 1. List the things Paul tells the Philippians to think about.

👁 2. What does Paul tell the Philippians to practice?

👁 3. What will be the result of practicing these things?

✦ 4. What does it mean for something to be true?

✦ 5. What does it mean for something to be honorable?

✦ 6. What does "just" mean?

✦ 7. What does "pure" mean?

✦ 8. What does "lovely" mean?

✦ 9. What does "commendable" mean?

✦ 10. What does "excellent" and "worthy of praise" mean?

✦ 11. Who embodies all of these characteristics perfectly?

✦ 12. What is Paul telling the Philippians to do when he says "think about these things"?

✦ 13. What have the Philippians learned, received, heard and seen in Paul?

✦ 14. What do verses 8 and 9 have to do with each other?

✦ 15. Does verse 9 remind you of any previous verses we have studied?

✦ 16. Why would God's presence be a result of practicing Paul's teaching and example?

✦ 17. How are these verses related to verses 4 to 7?

♥ 18. What practical steps can you take to help you dwell more on what (and WHO) is true, honorable, just, pure, lovely, commendable, excellent and worthy of praise?

♥ 19. In what areas do you struggle to put into practice Paul's teaching and example?

♥ 20. How can verses 4 to 7 help you in putting these things into practice?

♥ 21. Do you ever feel that the God of peace is not with you? Examine your life to see if there is an area in which you are not obedient. Go back to verses 4 to 7. Don't be anxious, but present your requests to God with thanksgiving.

Day 5

Pray that the Lord would increase his presence in your life and give you more joy.

Read Philippians 4:2-9.

✦ 1. Paul writes about joy 12 times throughout this letter: 1:3, 8, 25; 2:2, 17, 18, 28, 29; 3:1; 4:1, 4, 10. He writes about his own joy even in the midst of suffering, and he repeatedly tells the Philippians to have joy in the midst of persecution. What are the reasons, either stated or implied in the above 12 verses, that Paul gives for having joy?

✦ 2. Why do you think Paul emphasizes joy so much?

♥ 3. If you are a follower of Christ, what reasons do you have for joy?

♥ 4. Give praise to God that because of what Jesus has done on the cross you can enjoy his presence and have joy that is not dependent on any circumstances.

Philippians 4:10-23

Day 1 - Review

Pray.

Review your notes from week 8.

Read Philippians 4:2-9.

✦ 1. Sum up what you learned last week.

❤ 2. If you are a follower of Jesus, do you recognize the need for your heart and mind to be guarded in Christ Jesus? Do you remind yourself of the peace that you have with God, purchased on the cross? How does dwelling on the gospel help you with anxiety?

❤ 3. How would your daily life change if your mind was more focused on the things of verse 8 and, ultimately, the Lord Jesus Christ?

♥ 4. Christian, do you have enough joy in your life? If not, dwell on the Lord Jesus Christ and what he has done to secure your citizenship in heaven.

Day 2

Pray.

Read Philippians 4.

Read Philippians 4:10-20.

Read verses 10 and 14-16.

👁 1. What caused Paul to rejoice in the Lord greatly?

👁 2. Skipping to verse 14: What did the Philippians do that was kind?

👁 3. What did the Philippians do that no other church did?

👁 4. What did the Philippians do when Paul was in Thessalonica?

👁 5. How many times did the Philippians send help to Paul?

✦ 6. What are verses 10 and 14-16 about?

✦ 7. How are these verses related to chapter 1:3-5?

✦ 8. How long have the Philippians been in partnership with Paul?

✦ 9. Read Acts 17:1-10. What was some of the fruit of the Philippians' support of Paul in Thessalonica?

♥ 10. How are you in financial partnership with others in the gospel? (Are you a member of a church where you regularly give? Do you encourage your church to use their resources for the advancement of the gospel, promoting evangelism and missions?)

♥ 11. Do you pray regularly that from the money that you give the Lord will bring eternal fruit through advancing the gospel? If not, figure out a plan to pray regularly and specifically for the missionaries and other supported workers of your church.

Day 3

Pray.

Read Philippians 4:10-23.

Read verses 11-13.

👁 1. Is Paul writing to the Philippians about their support and concern because he is in need?

👁 2. Why is Paul not in need? What has he learned?

👁 3. What does Paul know?

👁 4. What has Paul learned to face?

👁 5. What is the secret to being content that Paul has learned?

✦ 6. What does it mean to be content?

✦ 7. In what circumstances is Paul discontent?

✦ 8. How do previous verses in Philippians give evidence that Paul knows how to be content?

✦ 9. Who does the "him" refer to in verse 13?

✦ 10. How do you think Christ strengthens Paul in hunger and need?

✦ 11. Why would Paul write about being content in plenty and abundance? Isn't it easy to be content when circumstances are good?

✦ 12. Verse 13 is often taken out of context and used to support the ability of Christians to do various miracles or take on some ministry for which the person is too busy or ill-equipped. What does this verse mean in context? In other words, how is it related to the previous verses about being content? (What are the "all things" that Paul can do through Christ who strengthens him?) See 2 Corinthians 12:9-10.

♥ 13. In which circumstances or areas of life do you find it hardest to be content? Examine the following areas:

> ♥ Marriage: In what ways do you want your husband to change before you will be happy in your marriage?

> ♥ Singleness: In what ways do you think marriage will make you truly happy?

♥ Children: Do you worry about your children or become frustrated with their behavior and think life will be better when they are older or change? Or are you waiting to have children to be truly happy?

♥ Health?

♥ Financial Difficulties or Financial Abundance?

♥ Family Relationships?

♥ Career?

♥ Church?

♥ Living Arrangements?

♥ 14. Thinking about Paul's focus in life, how does your focus need to shift to result in your being content?

♥ 15. What things can you do throughout the day to shift your focus from yourself to Christ and his Kingdom? (Do verses 2-9 help with this?)

Day 4

Pray.

Read through Philippians 4:10-23.

Read verses 11-13.

Review the observation questions from Day 3.

✦ 1. Remembering verse 13 in context, what does it mean to "do all things through Christ"?

✦ 2. How does Christ strengthen his followers? Reread Philippians 3:10 and 4:19, and read Ephesians 3:16-20.

✦ 3. How can a follower of Christ strive to do all things through him, relying on his strength? Reread Philippians 2:5-8 and 4:6-9.

❤ 4. What are areas of your life where you are doing things in your own strength, not through Christ who strengthens you?

❤ 5. What ways can you strive to do all things through Christ, relying on his strength?

Pray.

Read Philippians 4:10-23.

Read verses 17-20.

👁 1. What does Paul not seek?

👁 2. What does Paul seek?

👁 3. What has Paul received?

👁 4. How is Paul's supply?

👁 5. What did Paul receive from Epaphroditus?

👁 6. How are the Philippians' gifts described?

👁 7. What will Paul's God do?

👁 8. Out of what will God supply the Philippians' needs?

✦ 9. What do you think the fruit is that increases to the Philippians' credit?

✦ 10. From whom will the Philippians get credit?

✦ 11. Why do you think Paul seeks "the fruit that increases to [the Philippians'] credit" more than the gift?

✦ 12. What does Paul mean when he writes that he has received "full payment and more"? Full payment for what?

✦ 13. What makes the gifts the Philippians sent through Epaphroditus "a fragrant offering, a sacrifice acceptable and pleasing to God"?

✦ 14. What kinds of needs will God supply? See Psalm 23 and 2 Corinthians 9:8.

✦ 15. Aren't there Christians who suffer from hunger, hardship, and pain? How is God supplying their needs? (Is verse 19 promising comfort based on financial giving?)

✦ 16. What kind of riches are there in glory in Christ Jesus? (Think about all that you have studied in Philippians.)

♥ 17. Does the advancement of the gospel as a result of your giving excite you? How can you use your money in ways that bear eternal fruit?

♥ 18. Pray for your money to bear fruit for the Kingdom. Make it a point to pray this every time you give.

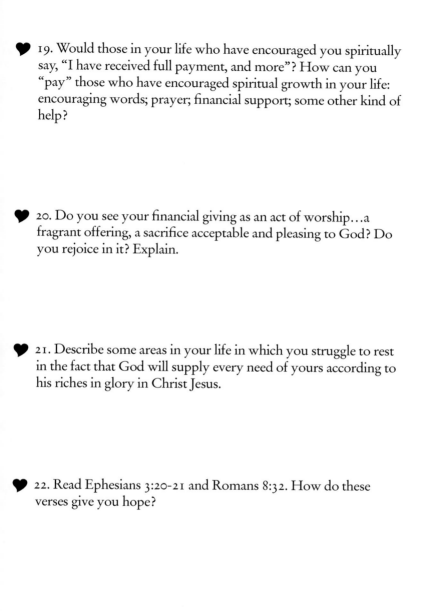

19. Would those in your life who have encouraged you spiritually say, "I have received full payment, and more"? How can you "pay" those who have encouraged spiritual growth in your life: encouraging words; prayer; financial support; some other kind of help?

20. Do you see your financial giving as an act of worship…a fragrant offering, a sacrifice acceptable and pleasing to God? Do you rejoice in it? Explain.

21. Describe some areas in your life in which you struggle to rest in the fact that God will supply every need of yours according to his riches in glory in Christ Jesus.

22. Read Ephesians 3:20-21 and Romans 8:32. How do these verses give you hope?

Read verses 20-23.

👁 23. To whom be the glory?

👁 24. For how long does God deserve the glory?

👁 25. To whom does Paul send greetings?

👁 26. Who greets the Philippians besides Paul?

👁 27. Whose grace does Paul pray will be with the Philippians?

✦ 28. Why do you think Paul puts verse 20 here?

✦ 29. Why are the greetings at the end of the letter important?

✦ 30. What is "the grace of the Lord Jesus Christ"?

✦ 31. What does it mean for that grace to be "with your spirit"?

♥ 32. What do these greetings teach us about loving one another in the church?

♥ 33. Verse 20 sums up Paul's philosophy of life. He wants God to get glory in every circumstance. It is what he lives for. In many ways, Philippians is a letter telling the church how to bring glory to God. Is this the philosophy for your life? If you are a Christian, praise God that he has saved you so that you can bring him glory. Pray that you and your church would be all about bringing glory to God.

♥ 34. If you are not a Christian, take time to examine your heart. Can you think of anything better than bringing glory to the one true God who created the universe? If you want this kind of life, all it takes is turning from your sin and putting your trust in Jesus Christ, who died for sinners. If you want to learn more about Jesus, who he is and what he has done, read through the Gospel of Mark and talk to a friend who already knows Jesus.

This week we will review the letter to the Philippians, but let's begin by reviewing what we learned last week.

Pray.

Read Philippians 4:10-23.

Review your notes from week 9.

✦ 1. What is the main point Paul is making in verses 10-13?

♥ 2. When you find discontentedness in your heart, what will you do?

✦ 3. What is the main point that Paul is making in verses 14-20?

♥ 4. How do these verses give you hope?

Day 2

Today we will begin our review of the entire letter to the Philippians.

Pray for the Lord to write the truth of his word on your heart.

Remind yourself of the context of the letter:

👁 1. What are the circumstances in Paul's life when he writes the letter?

👁 2. What is going on in the lives of the saints of Philippi (the church) when Paul writes the letter?

👁 3. What is the overall tone of the letter?

👁 4. Why did Paul write this letter to the church at Philippi?

Read through Philippians 1-4 in one sitting. Review your study notes.

✦ 5. What are the themes or the main points of Philippians?

Pray.

Over the next few days, there will be a series of questions to remind us how to apply the Scripture to your life. We've already gone through Philippians in detail and asked application questions. Now is our chance to be reminded of what we have learned and look for our greatest areas of need. Be in prayer as you apply these truths to your life.

Review the main points you wrote down yesterday. Then answer the following questions:

♥ 1. Did I learn something new about God, his ways, his character, his plans, and his priorities? If so, how should I be living as a result of this truth?

♥ 2. Do I need to change my beliefs based on a passage in Philippians, or is a truth reinforced?

♥ 3. Is there a particular behavior I need to adopt or stop?

Day 4

Pray that the Lord will continue to apply the truths of Scripture to your heart.

Review the main points you wrote on day 2. Go back to the text of Scripture often as you apply the main points. Answer the following questions:

♥ 1. Does Philippians have implications for the way I should relate to the church?

♥ 2. Does Philippians have implications for the way I relate to or speak to my non-Christian friends?

♥ 3. How should I pray based on what I have learned studying Philippians?

Pray that the Lord will continue to apply the truths of Scripture to your heart.

Review the main points you wrote on day 2. Go back to the text of Scripture often as you apply the main points. Answer the following questions:

♥ 1. Should I be praising God for something?

♥ 2. Do I see a sin for which I need to repent?

♥ 3. Is there an encouragement or promise on which I need to dwell?

♥ 4. The letter to the Philippians exudes joy even in the midst of difficult circumstances because both Paul and the Philippian Christians consider knowing Jesus to surpass any earthly value. They are in partnership together to serve and proclaim the glory of this great Lord and King for whom every knee will bow and every tongue confess. May you have this same joy as you "press on toward the goal for the prize of the upward call of God in Christ Jesus."

More Books from Cruciform Press

The Organized Heart: A Woman's Guide to Conquering Chaos, by Staci Eastin

Modest: Men and Women Clothed in the Gospel, by R W Glenn, Tim Challies

Intentional Parenting: Family Discipleship by Design, by Tad Thompson

Friends and Lovers: Cultivating Companionship & Intimacy in Marriage, by Joel R. Beeke

Brass Heavens: Reasons for Unanswered Prayer, by Paul Tautges

Grieving, Hope, and Solace: When a Loved One Dies in Christ, by Albert N. Martin

Cruciform: Living the Cross-Shaped Life, by Jimmy Davis

Innocent Blood: Challenging the Powers of Death with the Gospel of Life, by John Ensor

Reclaiming Adoption: Missional Living Through the Rediscovery of Abba Father, by Dan Cruver, John Piper, Scotty Smith, Richard D. Phillips, Jason Kovacs